ROBOTS!

Draw Your Own Androids, Cyborgs & Fighting Bots

Jay Stephens

LARK BOOKS

ing Publishing Co., Inc.
New York / London

Library of Congress Cataloging-in-Publication Data

Stephens, Jay.
  Robots! : draw your own androids, cyborgs &
    fighting bots / Jay Stephens. --
1st ed.
    p. cm.
  ISBN-13: 978-1-57990-937-6 (pb-trade pbk. : alk. paper)
  ISBN-10: 1-57990-937-X (pb-trade pbk. : alk. paper)
  1. Robots--Design and construction. I. Title.
  TJ211.15.S75 2007
  743'.89629892--dc22

                        2007027637

10 9 8 7 6 5 4 3 2 1

First Edition

Published by Lark Books, A Division of Sterling Publishing Co., Inc.
387 Park Avenue South, New York, N.Y. 10016

Text & Illustrations © 2008, Jay Stephens

Distributed in Canada by Sterling Publishing, c/o Canadian Manda Group, 165 Dufferin
Street, Toronto, Ontario, Canada M6K 3H6

Distributed in the United Kingdom by GMC Distribution Services,
Castle Place, 166 High Street, Lewes, East Sussex, England BN7 1XU

Distributed in Australia by Capricorn Link (Australia) Pty Ltd.,
P.O. Box 704, Windsor, NSW 2756 Australia

If you have questions or comments about this book, please contact:
Lark Books, 67 Broadway, Asheville, NC 28801 (828) 253-0467

Manufactured in China

ISBN 13: 978-1-57990-937-6
ISBN 10: 1-57990-937-X

For information about custom editions, special sales, premium and
corporate purchases, please contact Sterling Special Sales Department
at 800-805-5489 or specialsales@sterlingpub.com.

Editor
VERONIKA ALICE GUNTER

Creative Director
CELIA NARANJO

Art Director
ROBIN GREGORY

Contents

FUNCTIONAL FORMS

PEEOOOWWWWWW!

CYBER COLOR

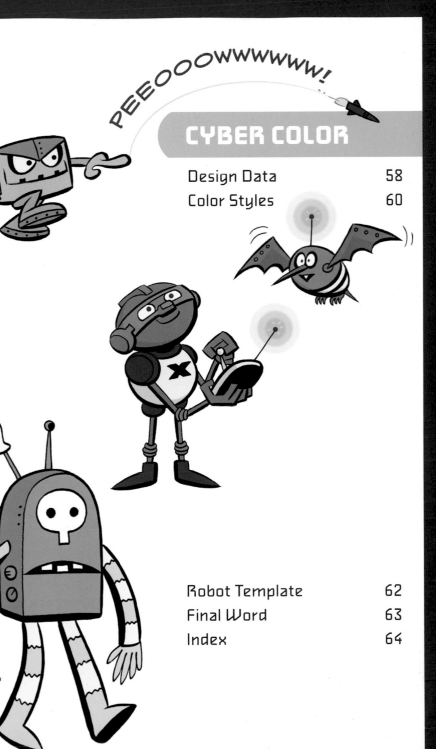

INDUSTRIAL EXTRAS

Robotics 101

Ready to invent a team of fierce fighting bots? Maybe you'd prefer a friendly doting android that does all of your chores and plays your favorite games? If you don't have a blowtorch and a half-ton of steel, you can create robots with paper and pencil!

A robot is any machine built and programmed to do whatever its creator wants. You may want to draw robots like the ones you see in movies, cartoons, comic books, and on cards. Or you can invent a robot of your very own. I'll show you how to draw any kind of robot you can imagine.

Every page in this book is full of ideas and techniques for creating technologically talented toys and programmable pals. I've included a bunch of my favorite inventions to guide you along. The instructions will help you develop your drawing skills—and stretch your imagination.

Drawing is Easy

You'll use the pencil to lightly draw simple shapes and lines on your paper—zigzags, circles, straight lines, and curved ones. (I call these construction lines.) You'll be doing exactly what industrial designers do when they invent new cars, buildings, and gadgets! Then trace over your best drawings with the pen or marker. (I call this inking the final drawing.) Then you use the eraser to get rid of the lines you aren't using. (That's why none of your marks have to be perfect—but you do need to draw them lightly so they erase easily.) There are lots of ways to add color to your final drawings. I put a section about it at the end of the book.

Learning how to make marks on paper is only part of drawing. But it's true that the more you doodle, the better you'll get. So use this book and draw a lot! Just remember: your imagination is the most important part of making anything, especially a robot. Think about what you want your robot to do, how it looks, and how it's powered. Then use what I show you to draw your own robots!

—Jay Stephens

To set up your robotics lab, you will need:

- Some plain, white paper (8½ x 11-inch computer paper works well)

- A regular 2H, HB, or 2B pencil (a school pencil works, too)

- A pen or fine-tipped marker (black, if possible, but dark blue will do)

- A good eraser (gum or plastic are best)

- Colored markers, pencils, or water-based paints, and/or a scanner and a computer with illustration software

Most people think of robots, androids, and cyborgs as recent inventions. But people have been imagining and building mechanical beings for thousands of years.

Talos was a giant bronze robot from ancient Greek mythology. It had the face and body of a man wearing a helmet and armor. Arrows and spears bounced off Talos as he guarded the island of Crete.

The word "robot" was coined in 1923. It came from the English translation of Czech writer Karl Capek's play *R.U.R.* about androids that revolt against their cruel masters. Robota means forced labor in Czech. Capek's androids were called Robots.

Writer L. Frank Baum created **Nick Chopper** more than 100 years ago. Nick is better known as **The Tin Woodsman** that joined Dorothy on her quest to find the wonderful Wizard of Oz.

Will your robot have multiple heads, or none at all? How about just a head with legs?

Heads

Garganto is a steam-powered wrecking crew with seating for one right on top of its metal skull. Garganto's eyes shine high-power lights so its operator can see in the dark. Its big jaw is for crunching rubble for fuel.

There's no better place to start thinking about your robot than in your head!

Look all around—inspiring shapes are everywhere. This four-slice toaster looks a little depressed!

Big head? Or just a little noggin?
You decide when you design your original robots!

A round or oval head appears more human. Do you want your robot to look like a person?

Here's a sharp look.

A square noggin is definitely more machine-like.

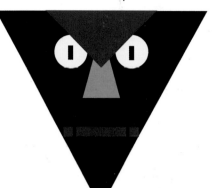

What if the body was the head?

Mix up a bunch of shapes for a far-out head. Use a ruler if you want perfect straight lines.

Will your robot think? Will it have a brain, a computer and programs, or an operator that tells it what to do?

Sensors

Will your robot detect and respond to motion, sound, light, or heat? Then it will need sensors. Any kind you can imagine!

FXIVR-2885 doesn't have a mouth or nose, or sense of touch. It makes up for all that with super-sensitive sonar ears and a scanner that can see through anything!

Now, let's have a ball with some eye-like sensors!

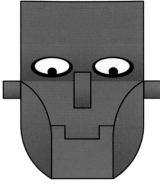

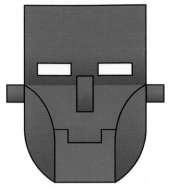

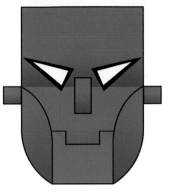

Round or oval eyes with pupils look friendly and humanoid.

Square and rectangular eyes look mechanical—and a little spooky.

Triangular eyes set at an angle are sinister and angry...yikes!

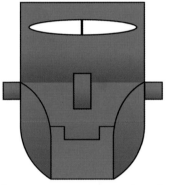

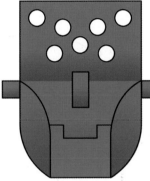

Why not try a bunch of eyes, like a spider?

One eye is enough, right?

Googly, far-apart eyes look silly and harmless.

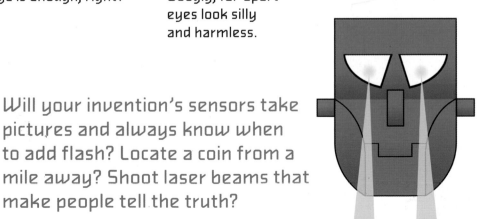

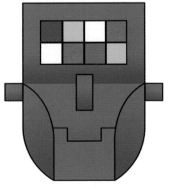

Will your invention's sensors take pictures and always know when to add flash? Locate a coin from a mile away? Shoot laser beams that make people tell the truth?

More Sensors

These antennae are simple "L" shapes with dots on the ends.

How about satellite dish ears?

Here's a triangle nose, half dark and half light.

This robot has triangular funnels that hear, see, and smell.

This hose nose can squirt, grab, and sniff!

Why not get animal inspiration and try rabbit ears? What will they do?

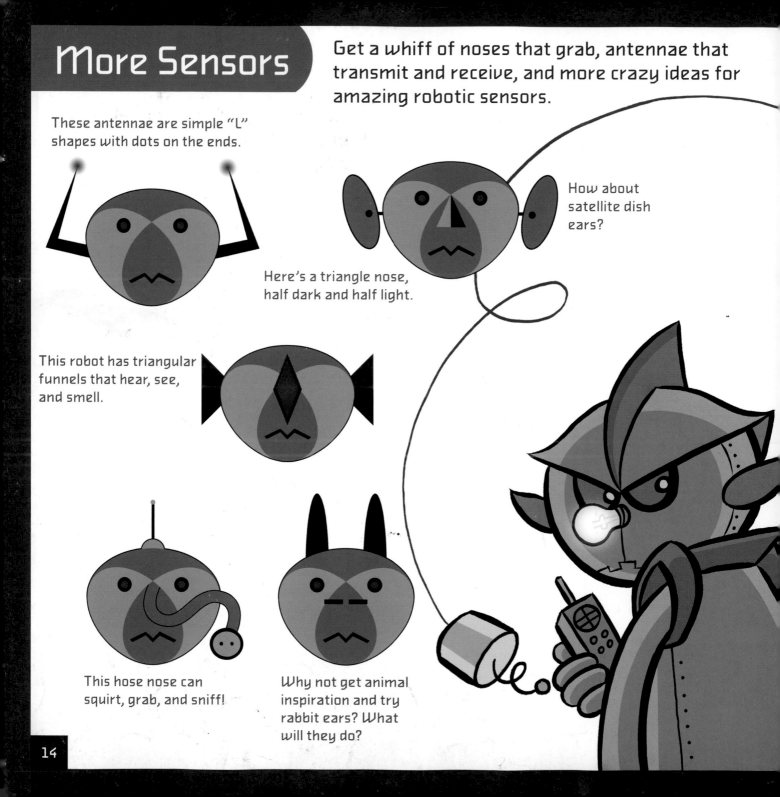

This contraption has a neat-o aerial that picks up your favorite radio signals.

How many sensors are too many?

Are they freckles or air monitors that detect rotten smells?

Snoop is trying to listen in on **Meteor Mike's** secret conversation. Can you think of a sneakier way for your robot to spy?

Communicators

How will your inventions communicate with you? Bite into these ideas for mouth-like voice boxes, loud speakers, and cyber-chompers.

Give a bionic buddy a unique voice by drawing an unusual word balloon or printing special letters.

You said it!

A straight-line mouth that curves up at the ends looks happy.

A zigzag snappy jaw.

Downward curves at the corners create a sad or glum look.

A circle mouth communicates a surprised "Oh!"

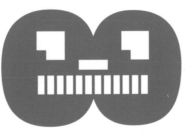

Want some pearly whites? Draw lots of vertical lines for a teeth-like grill.

Of course, a robot doesn't need a mouth. Yours might beep when it blinks or send you mental messages.

A profile is the outline of the head from the side. A "V" shape and a "C" shape are both easy to draw for mouths.

Connections

Some assembly required!

B

D

C

E

A

F

G

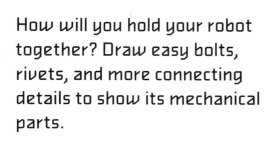

How will you hold your robot together? Draw easy bolts, rivets, and more connecting details to show its mechanical parts.

A rivet is a nail with a flattened head that's driven into metal. Robots can have rivets anywhere their parts connect. Draw a rivet with a small circle, a sideways "C" shape, or a little dot.

Hi! I just bolted from the laboratory!

Don't look so shocked! Visible wiring is a great way to show how a robot's electrical system works. Just draw lines. This guy is plugged in.

BOING!

BZZT!

Don't go nuts trying to get your fasteners just right. Here's how:

Ready to draw some robots? Here are a couple of inventions to get you started...

BUILD IT!

Use what you know to draw this simple robot friend.

AUTOMA TOM

PURPOSE: Provide companionship and comfort to anyone without brothers or sisters.

SPECIAL FUNCTIONS: Tom can walk you to school, help with home-work, and play games with you. It's also a good listener—it has sensors that both hear and feel what you say. Unlike human siblings, Tom never argues.

 1. Draw a rectangle for Tom's head. Add two evenly spaced sideways "C" humps on the top. These are light communicators.

A long, wide "C" curve for the neck

4. Add curved lines to the communicators, ears, and neck. The nose is a rectangle with a little square at one end.

Three dots on each cheek—rivet freckles!

Draw teeth with just three short lines each.

2. Draw an oval on one side of the rectangle and a long "C" curve on the other. Now it looks like a tube.

3. A small oval and "C" shape make ear-like feeling sensors. The eyes are circles. A "C" shape plus short lines create a smile.

Lines attach this ear.

Erase the lines you don't need.

5. Create your final drawing by tracing your best construction lines with a pen or marker.

6. Color away! A lighter streak makes Tom's metal head gleam.

Erase the lighter lines or just color over them.

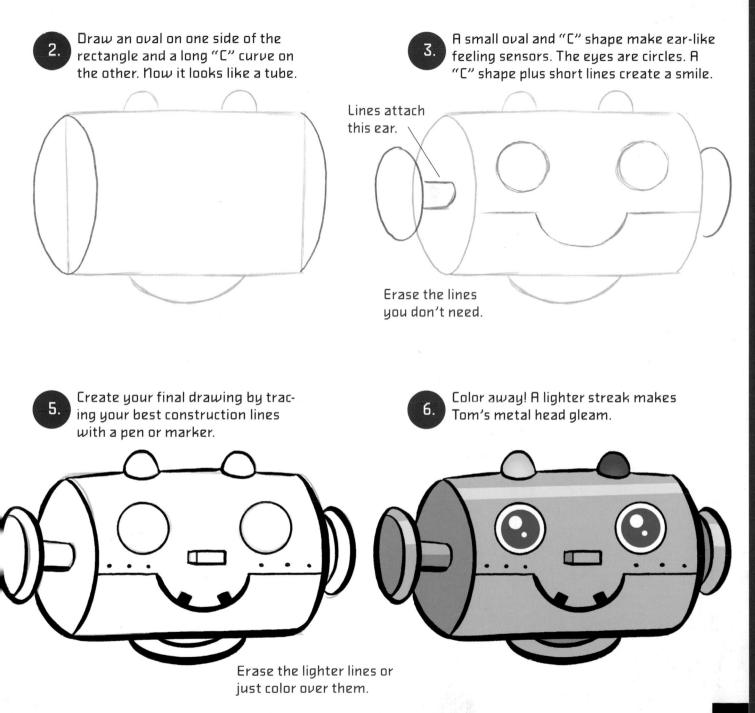

BUILD IT!

Spaceflight bandits beware!

CYBORELLA

PURPOSE: Ensure comfort and safety on intergalactic flights.

SPECIAL FUNCTIONS: Cyborella is a safety officer. It serves food and beverages, recharges battery-operated gadgets, and keeps its mesmerizing X-ray-vision eyes on everyone. Cyborella hypnotizes trouble-makers by blinking at them.

1. Start with an egg-shape. Sketch two lines to help place Cyborella's humanoid facial features.

The lines intersect closer to this side of the head.

This side of the oval is a little flat.

4. Finish the ear bolt with a small oval, a "C" shape, and a line.

A stretched-out "S" line finishes the helmet.

Create metallic reflections with simple lines.

A boxy "U" shape plus straight lines create each neck segment.

2. Draw two slanted ovals for the eyes.

A circle for the ear bolt

A tiny triangle nose

Two curved lines with a line between them for lips

3. Make Cyborella's metal hairline with a curving "M" shape that dips down at the middle sketch line. An upside down "V" finishes each eye.

A "J" curve hair helmet

Two sloping lines form the neck.

5. Use a dark-colored pen or marker to trace your best construction lines.

Erase the lines you drew in pencil.

6. Color Cyborella!

A little shading looks cool.

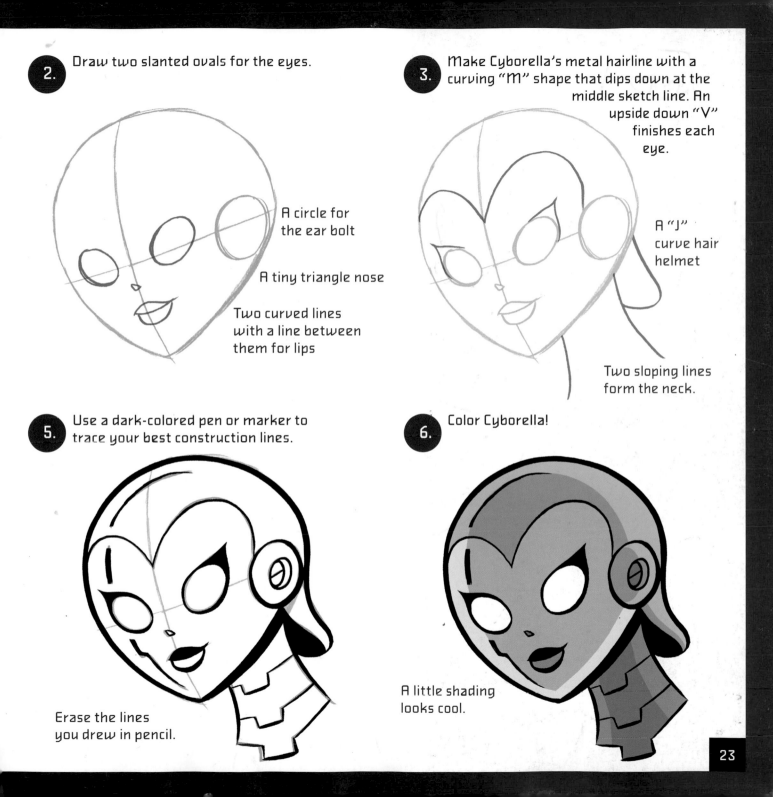

FUNCTIONAL FORMS design data

Some machines are designed in the form of a human or an animal. A Greek myth from the 8th century BC tells of robot watchdogs. **Kuon Khryseos** looked like a dog, down to its tail and teeth. But this tireless machine was made of solid gold—and almost impossible to damage or outrun!

Inventors know how to give a gizmo a body that helps it do its job, or look the part.

People design industrial robots to function efficiently. These bodies only include parts that help get the job done—fast and well.

Automaton means "self-operating machine" in Latin and "acting of its own free will" in Greek. More than one are called automata.

In the 1870s, Edward Ellis created **Steam Man** for a novel about an adventurous inventor and his robots. Steam Man's friendly human face and form put people at ease as it pulled them in wagons.

Karakuri ningyo are mechanical wooden puppets dating as far back as 18th-century Japan. They're toys used as actors in plays.

25

Body Construction

What's a good body for your robot? The kind that works!

POINTS
41

#1

Most robots are invented to make life easier for people. What do you want a robot to help you with? What body parts, tools, and accessories will it need?

BOING!

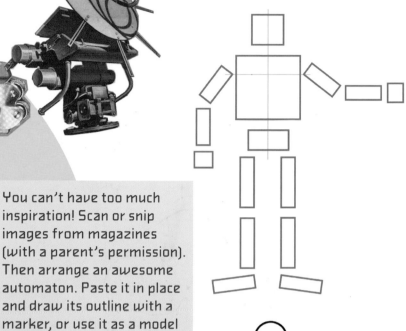

Want an android? Sketch out a basic human-like body shape using 15 blocks.

You can't have too much inspiration! Scan or snip images from magazines (with a parent's permission). Then arrange an awesome automaton. Paste it in place and draw its outline with a marker, or use it as a model for drawing.

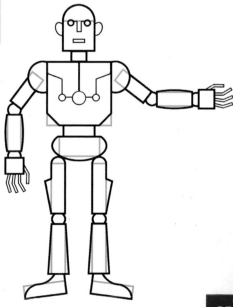

Arms

Give your invention any kind of arms you want. And any number of them, too.

Get a grip on this armload of ideas.

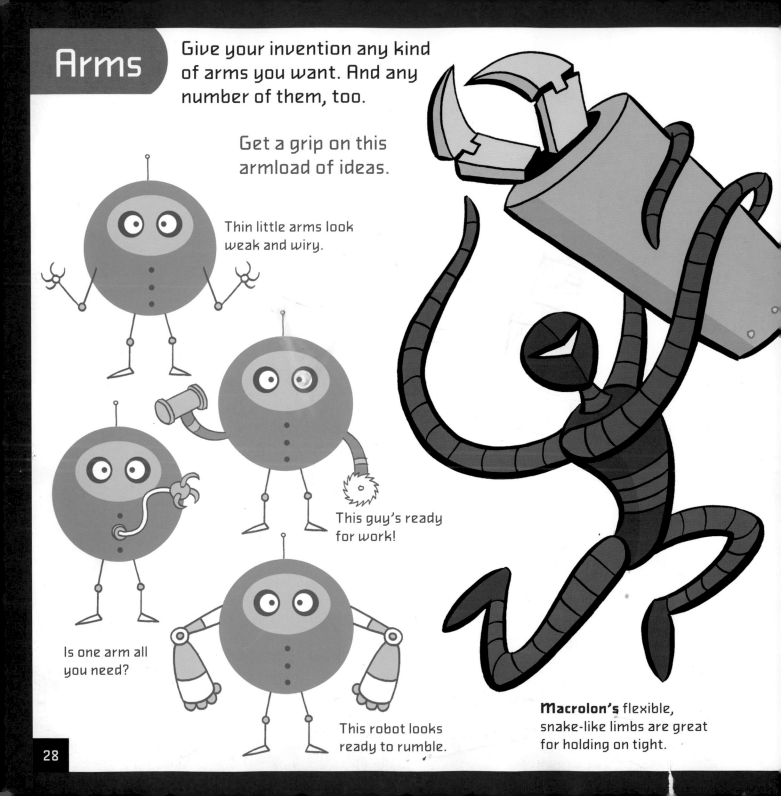

Thin little arms look weak and wiry.

This guy's ready for work!

Is one arm all you need?

This robot looks ready to rumble.

Macrolon's flexible, snake-like limbs are great for holding on tight.

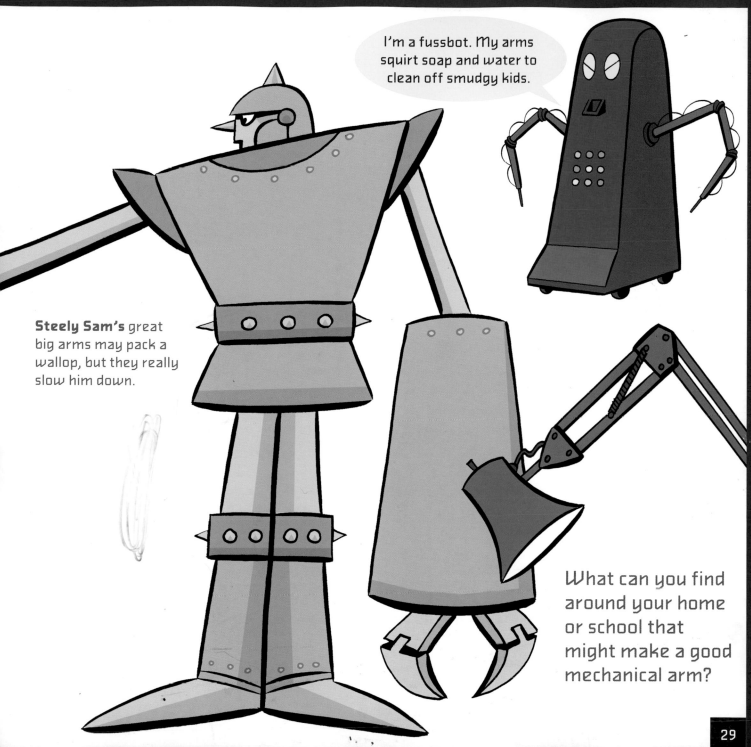

I'm a fussbot. My arms squirt soap and water to clean off smudgy kids.

Steely Sam's great big arms may pack a wallop, but they really slow him down.

What can you find around your home or school that might make a good mechanical arm?

Joints

Will your computerized chum have covered joints like a person, or exposed hinges so oiling and repairs are easy?

Elbows, knees, shoulders, and toes...a human body is full of hinges that you can't see. Let it inspire your robot's form!

A cyborg is a machine with human or animal parts. A person with electronic parts that give her superhuman ability is called bionic. Which do you think **Turbomax** is?

Squeeky here has so many joints that it needs to keep an oilcan in its chest compartment for rainy days when its joints get creaky. Can you think of a way to keep your robot dry so it won't rust?

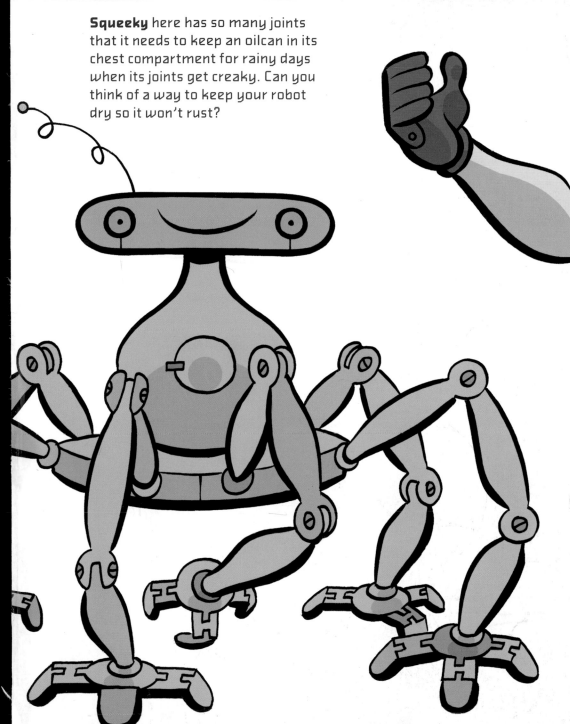

Find inspiration for mechanical joints in your room! How about an action figure? A door hinge?

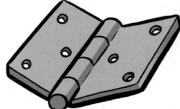

Does your robot need legs?

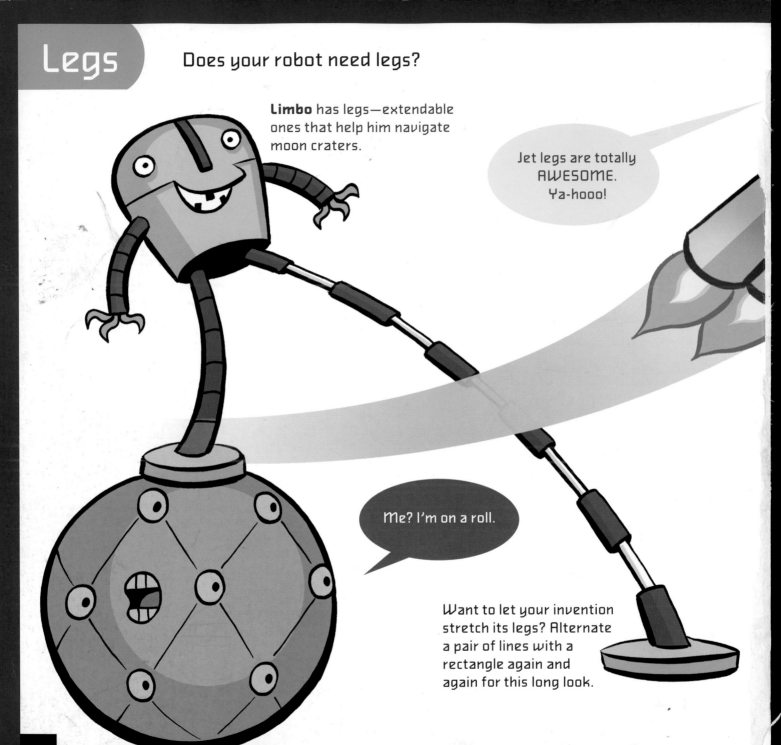

Limbo has legs—extendable ones that help him navigate moon craters.

Jet legs are totally AWESOME. Ya-hooo!

Me? I'm on a roll.

Want to let your invention stretch its legs? Alternate a pair of lines with a rectangle again and again for this long look.

All you need to build a simple leg are two rectangles for the upper and lower leg, a circle for the knee, and a triangle for the foot. Try it!

Sketch a pair of legs with four lines and two "V" shapes.

Some robots need nothing more than a couple of little legs to get around.

You might want legs that also work as hands!

Add two more lines for a knee.

Maybe your legs could transform? Into what?

How about a pair of battle boots?

Of course, robots can have as many knees as you please!

Wheels, wings, rockets, treads...
So many means of moving your machine!

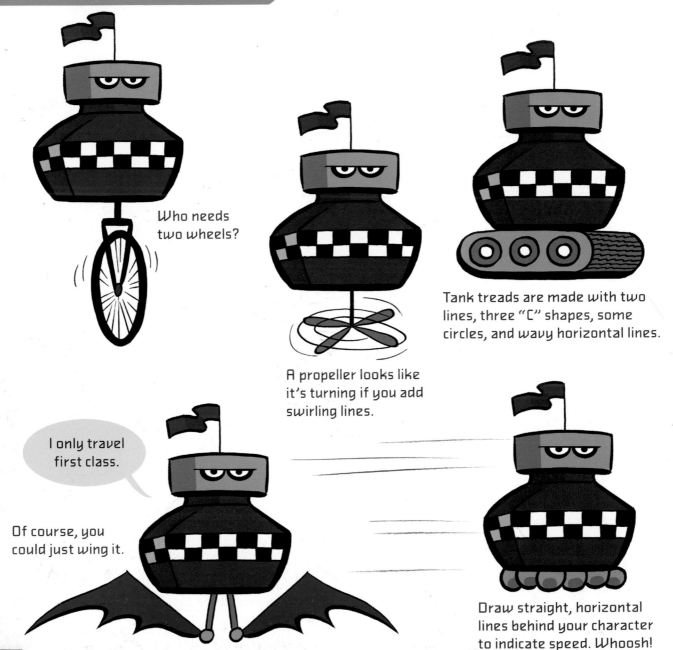

Who needs
two wheels?

A propeller looks like
it's turning if you add
swirling lines.

Tank treads are made with two
lines, three "C" shapes, some
circles, and wavy horizontal lines.

I only travel
first class.

Of course, you
could just wing it.

Draw straight, horizontal
lines behind your character
to indicate speed. Whoosh!

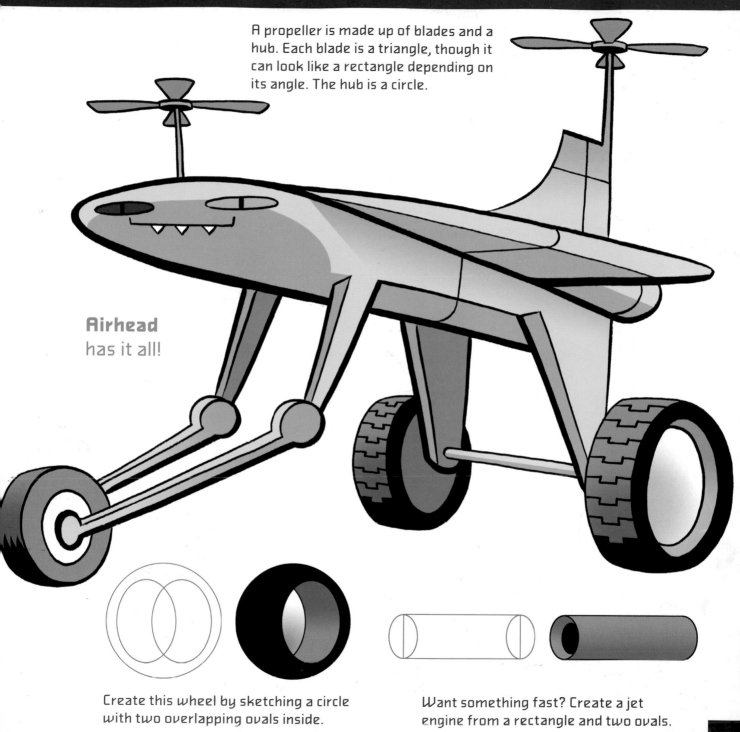

A propeller is made up of blades and a hub. Each blade is a triangle, though it can look like a rectangle depending on its angle. The hub is a circle.

Airhead
has it all!

Create this wheel by sketching a circle with two overlapping ovals inside.

Want something fast? Create a jet engine from a rectangle and two ovals.

Transforming Parts

Will your robot have hidden talents?

For messages that just have to be delivered in person, design a cell-phone robot that flies.

Cars, furniture, dinosaurs... What could a robot transform into? What advantage would this second identity give your gizmo?

Hopalong Trashidy changes from a kitchen waste bin into a bouncing bot that carries trash to the curb. Maybe you could reprogram it to collect the rubbish, too!

HOP! HOP!

Maybe only one part of your invention will transform.

This head easily shifts back to a little television set.

That's a lot of garbage.

Ready to draw some bot bodies?

BUILD IT!

Form a fully equipped mechanic from simple shapes.

GREASEMONKEY

PURPOSE: Build and repair robots. Provide maintenance services including oiling joints and recharging batteries.

SPECIAL FUNCTIONS: This robot diagnoses and corrects problems using internal gauges and tools. Each wrench-like arm can lift a ton. Greasemonkey's head-mounted radar detector picks up emergency beacons in 143,866 programming languages.

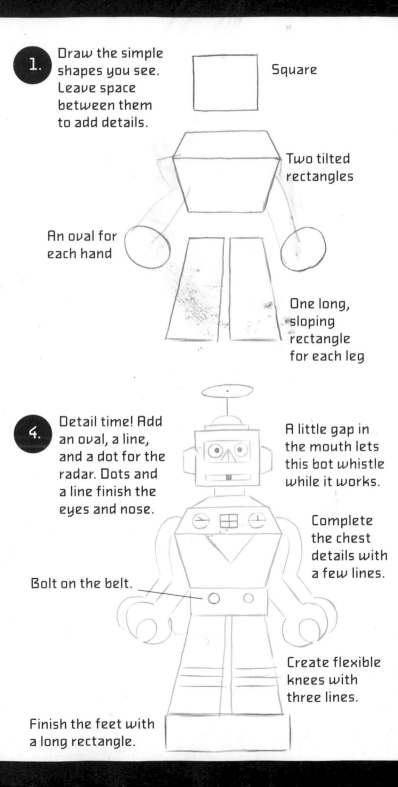

1. Draw the simple shapes you see. Leave space between them to add details.

Square

Two tilted rectangles

An oval for each hand

One long, sloping rectangle for each leg

4. Detail time! Add an oval, a line, and a dot for the radar. Dots and a line finish the eyes and nose.

A little gap in the mouth lets this bot whistle while it works.

Complete the chest details with a few lines.

Bolt on the belt.

Create flexible knees with three lines.

Finish the feet with a long rectangle.

2. Draw two rectangles inside the head and one on top.

Three lines for the upper chest

Upside-down "J" arms, plus a short line ending at each hand.

Join the chest and legs.

3. Use circles as eyes and round chest dials.

Triangle nose and chest detail

A "C" shape on top and a square-ish "C" shape on each side of the head

Two lines for the neck

Repeat the "J" shape outside each arm.

A "C" shape forms each hand.

5. Create your final drawing by tracing your best construction lines with a pen or marker.

Erase the lighter lines or color over them.

6. Color Greasemonkey!

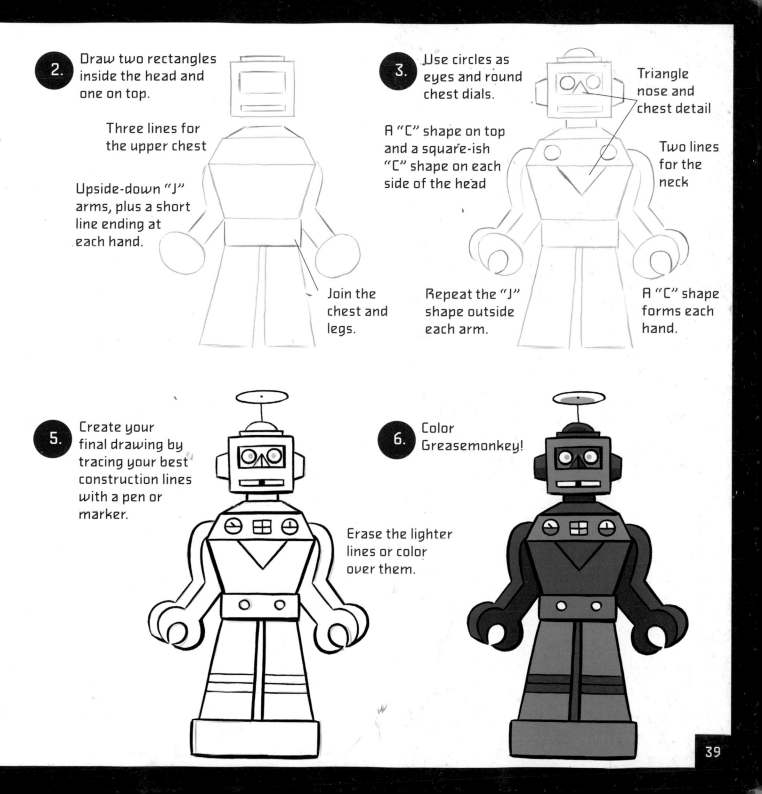

BUILD IT!

Use what you know to draw a fighting machine.

GOKIN 9

PURPOSE: Entertain humans by battling other robots in Mecha Wrestling Federation games.

SPECIAL FUNCTIONS: Gokin 9 has guided-missile fists that never miss, laser-dazer eye beams that disable a competitor's code, and magnetic stabilizers to keep it on its feet. Gokin 9 is remote controlled. It's also the reigning champion with 312 knock outs. Mecha wrestlers never destroy opponents or hurt people.

1. Begin with some chunky shapes.

Trapezoid chest

Smaller rectangle fist

Rectangle fist

Four short, straight lines form the shorts.

Long lines map out the legs.

4. It's all in the details! Draw two "L"s for each ear receiver. Connect each pair with a short line at the top.

Two curves shape the hips.

2. Draw an oval head with a line for the brow.

Two "C" curves and two lines make this arm.

Three lines for fingers

A "C" curve and one line form this arm.

Two curved lines for the feet

3. Sloping rectangles make the eyes and nose.

A small "C" on each finger

Create the belt and the boot tops with a wide, upside-down "V" for each.

5. Use a dark-colored pen or marker to trace your best construction lines.

Erase the extra lines.

6. Add color to finish this fighting bot.

For a metallic shine, combine dark shading and highlights.

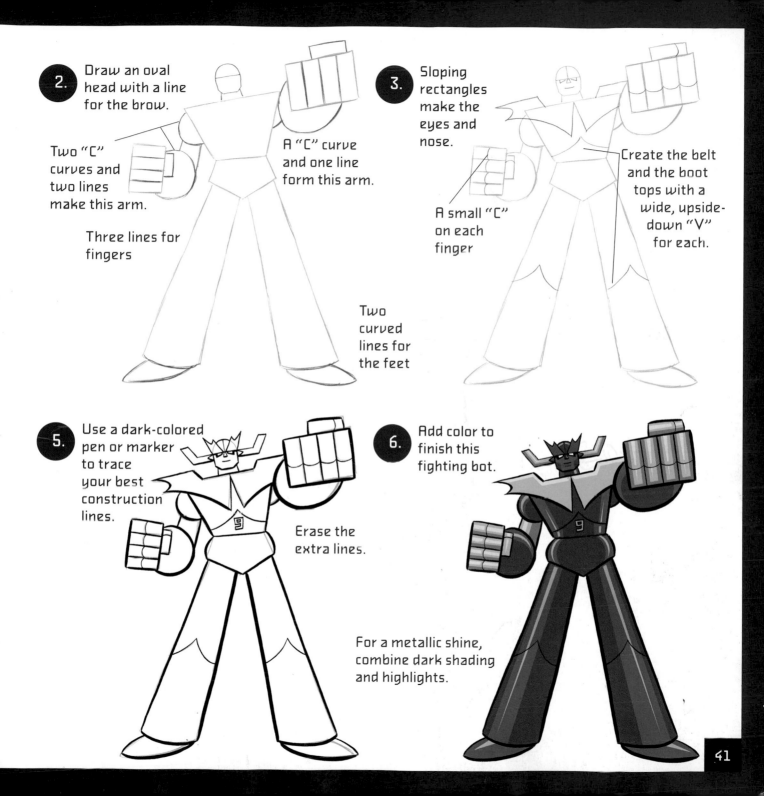

Final touches like these complete a robot's look, show how it's controlled, or hint at what it does.

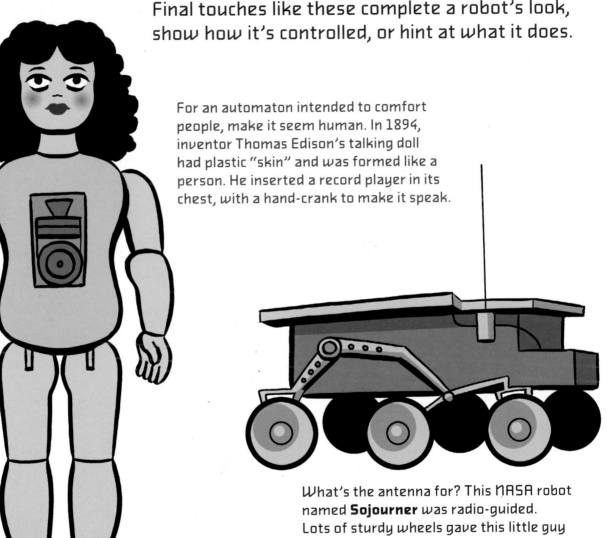

For an automaton intended to comfort people, make it seem human. In 1894, inventor Thomas Edison's talking doll had plastic "skin" and was formed like a person. He inserted a record player in its chest, with a hand-crank to make it speak.

What's the antenna for? This NASA robot named **Sojourner** was radio-guided. Lots of sturdy wheels gave this little guy plenty of traction as it roved the surface of the planet Mars in 1997.

Wind **Tick Tock** up under the left arm for thinking, under the right arm for speaking, and in his back for action. Tick Tock was an imaginary mechanical toy featured in the 1907 story *Ozma of Oz*.

The **Robot Knight** was designed by artist and inventor Leonardo Da Vinci more than 500 years ago. The metal casing would protect the cable-and-pulley gears that powered it.

1,000,000 X

Nanobots are so tiny, they work inside atoms and molecules. And they're real! These robots were created using nanotechnology, a science discovered within the last 50 years and conducted at the microscopic level.

Materials

Protect those delicate wires and circuit boards inside your robot! Do you need thick, heavy metal for tough jobs and rough conditions, or plastic to look like human skin?

Plastic, vinyl, and rubber can be any color and any shape.

Silver, copper, or another metal? Add a highlight to make it gleam.

Dents and scratches make metal look old or beat-up.

Slagg is made of Plutonian iron.

Ugene has plastic skin that feels just like flesh.

Use zigzag jigsaw lines to draw crystal or alien glass.

Combine a fiberglass skull with a soft rubber face for a tough robot with a humanoid appearance.

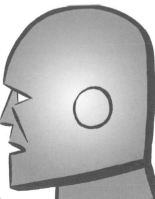

Who says your robot has to be made of something solid? This holographic head is made of light.

Gearzo has a human body, plus steel replacement parts for his feet and arm.

Armor

Shell, shield, breastplate, elbow pads...
Don't leave your bots unprotected!

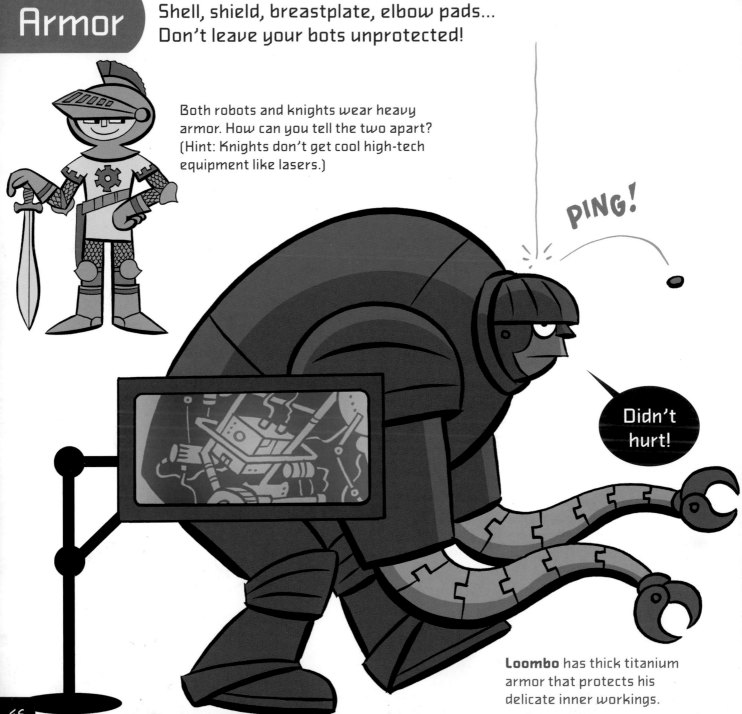

Both robots and knights wear heavy armor. How can you tell the two apart? (Hint: Knights don't get cool high-tech equipment like lasers.)

PING!

Didn't hurt!

Loombo has thick titanium armor that protects his delicate inner workings.

Metal makes great armor because it's strong—and the dents can be easily hammered out when your bot comes home damaged. What other hard materials could you use?

WHAM!

Armor can be offensive as well as defensive. Just ask **Whammo**!

Here are a few ways to draw segments of armor...

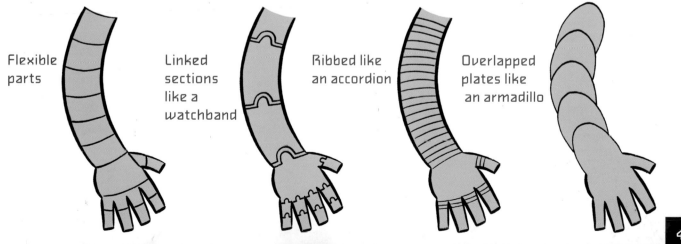

Flexible parts

Linked sections like a watchband

Ribbed like an accordion

Overlapped plates like an armadillo

Dials & Levers

Buttons, dials, switches, blinking lights, and other visible controls and gauges are easy to draw. Did you give your robot an "off" switch? If it malfunctions, you'll wish you had!

Try circle dials and rectangular or square gauges or levers.

You can trace coins for circles, or use rulers to get straight lines.

Could someone please switch me into high gear?

A radar or sonar detector needs two circles, four lines, and a dot for what's detected.

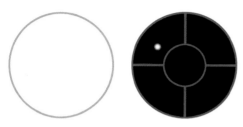

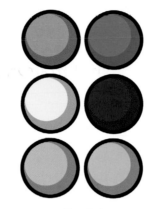

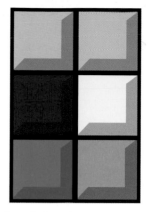

Make a complete control panel.

Push buttons and blinking lights look good as circles or square shapes.

1. Draw a square or rectangle.

2. Add a line, circles, a rectangle, and a square.

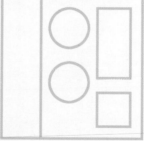

3. Fill in the shapes like you see here.

4. Add words or numbers as a final touch.

Defense Systems

Without weapons, cyborg superheroes, bionic crime fighters, and fighting bots are just giant toasters.

Shhhh!

Maybe your robot's best defense is a special ability. Can it turn invisible? Or hover silently?

Sarge has a huge cannon. It fires lasers, missiles, and grenades. Luckily for us, Sarge has been programmed not to hurt living things.

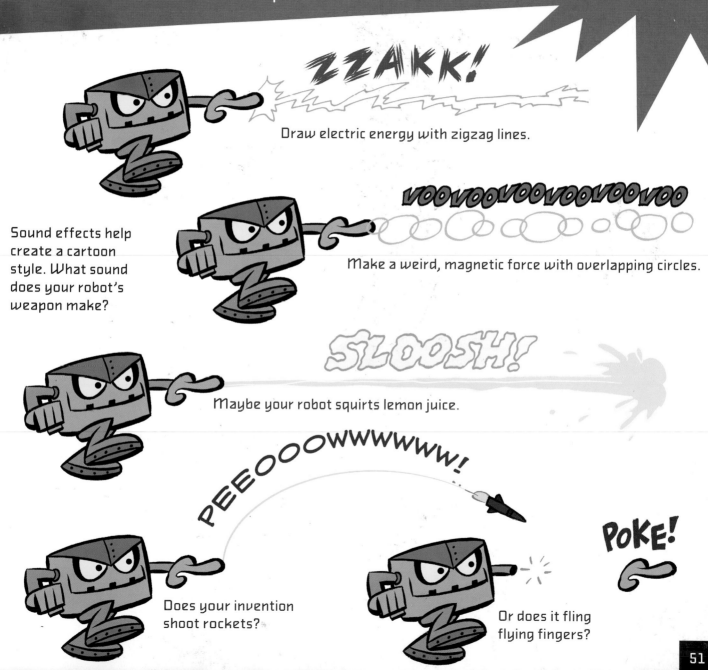

ZZAKK!

Draw electric energy with zigzag lines.

VOO VOO VOO VOO VOO VOO VOO

Sound effects help create a cartoon style. What sound does your robot's weapon make?

Make a weird, magnetic force with overlapping circles.

SLOOSH!

Maybe your robot squirts lemon juice.

PEEOOOWWWWWW!

Does your invention shoot rockets?

POKE!

Or does it fling flying fingers?

Controls

Will your robot be driven like a vehicle, operated from a distance, or left to its own devices?

Robots can work by remote-control. This is particularly helpful for secret spy robots.

Don't tell anyone—a little gray alien named **Foobler** hides inside the **Cosmotron** and controls its every move.

Some robots aren't controlled by anyone—they just do whatever they were programmed to do. Other mechanical folks do whatever they want. They might even do you a favor if you ask politely.

I say, you wouldn't mind helping me find my kitty cat, would you?

Certainly!

Here are simple controls for you to draw...

A steering wheel is all circles and curves.

A circle and rectangle create a radio you can use to give a robot voice commands.

A "B" shape turned on its side makes a video-game-style control.

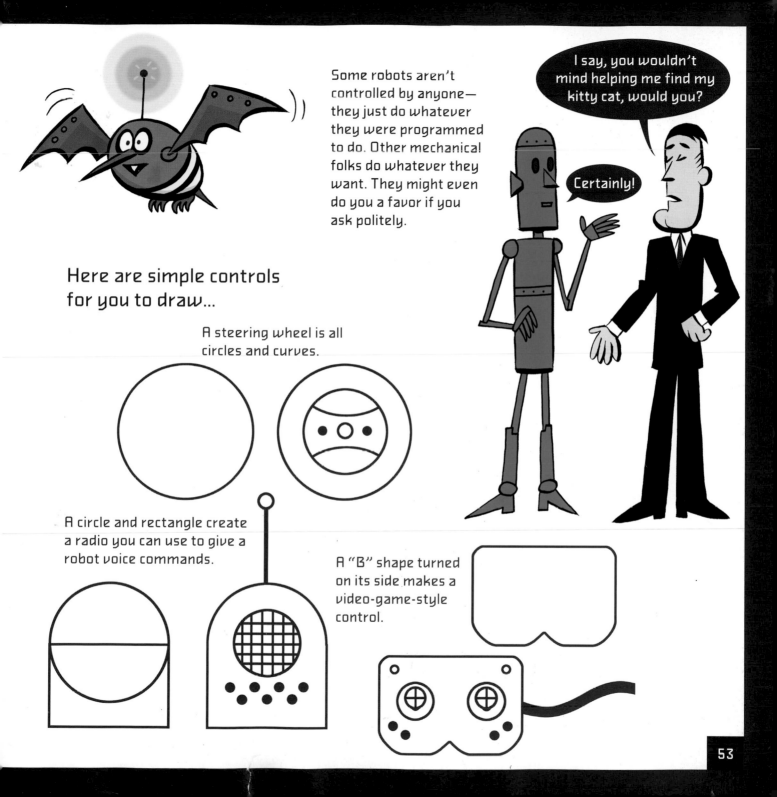

BUILD IT!

This android pop star has fans across the galaxy!

ASTRALUX

PURPOSE: Instruct humans and robots of all ages in music and voice. Compete in the annual Intergalactic Idol contest.

SPECIAL FUNCTIONS: Astralux has antennae-style tuning forks for a constantly on-key voice. Its left hand transforms into any musical instrument and is always perfectly tuned. Rocket feet guarantee a high-flying finale.

1. Begin with an oval head shape.

A circle and two "V" shapes

A smaller oval for the chest

Start the guitar-hand with four lines.

Two angled lines and an upside-down "V" create legs.

4. Add her antennae and finish the eyes.

Wrist-cuffs are two lines each.

More hair

Four more lines for boot tops

2. Add zigzags to make the hairline.

Tilted "V"s for eyes

A "C" neck

Little lines for eyebrows

A "W" guitar body

Four more lines and two "V"s for the legs and feet

Two lines mark off the belt.

3. Draw oval pupils, a curve smile, and a dot nose.

"C" shape fingers

"C" shape

Two short lines add shape to the pants and foot.

Add simple shapes to the guitar.

5. Ink your drawing.

Don't ink the "A" emblem if you want it white in your finished robot.

Erase your rough pencil lines.

6. Adding bright color sounds good to Astralux!

BUILD IT!

This bot is a top cop.

COPPER

PURPOSE: Protect fellow robots from dangerous criminals and sinister saboteurs—human or machine!

SPECIAL FUNCTIONS: Copper has an automatic crime detector, siren head, spectra-vision, and a sleep-ray and freeze-gas blaster. With its seven-day rechargeable battery, Copper can pursue suspects without taking a donut break.

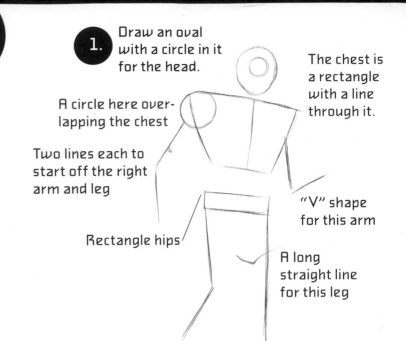

1. Draw an oval with a circle in it for the head.

The chest is a rectangle with a line through it.

A circle here overlapping the chest

Two lines each to start off the right arm and leg

"V" shape for this arm

Rectangle hips

A long straight line for this leg

4. Most of the last details are drawn with small curved "C" marks and circles.

Ears

A few lines will give you fingers.

Complete the legs and feet with three more lines.

A rectangle and upside-down triangle with a star make the badge.

2. Two lines for each ear nodule

"V" neck

"C" shape

Draw four small circles at the hips and elbows.

Two straight lines for the spine

Draw a slanted rectangle and triangle for the blaster.

3. Finish off the head and ears with some short curved lines.

Curved line

Neck lines

Straight lines and curves for the arms

Three circles

Two blocks for the hand

A few more straight lines complete the legs.

Four lines to draw the feet

5. Time to trace your light pencil drawing in dark pen or marker.

Erase any lines you aren't using.

6. Now add some arresting colors.

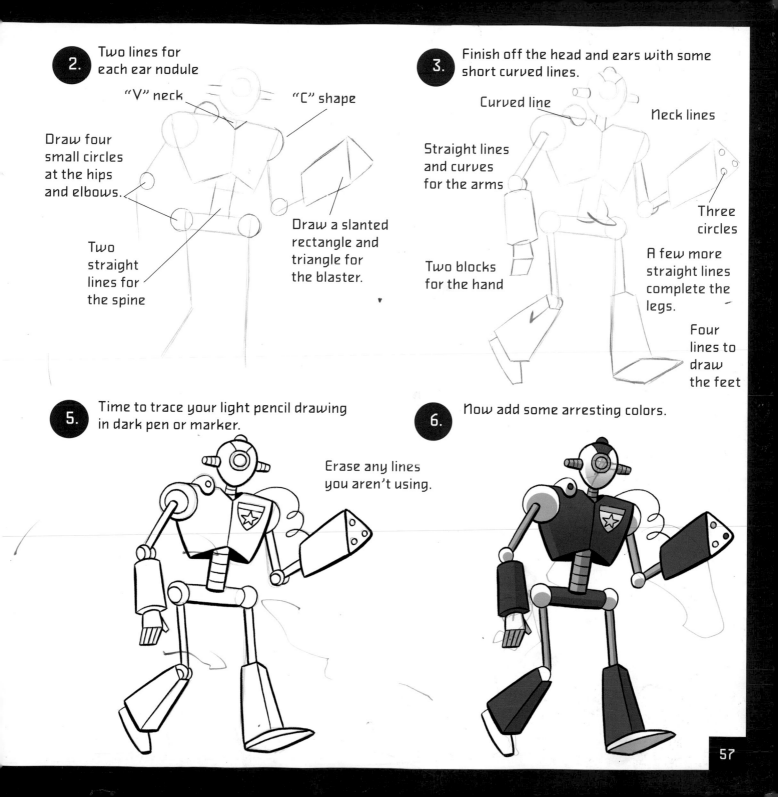

Cyber Color design data

Try these bright ideas for coloring the robots you create.

Green and orange are good colors for giant Martian war machines. This **Tripod** from the book *The War of the Worlds* has a cockpit for the pilot, plus steel tentacles and a lethal heat ray.

The side of the robot facing a light source is always brightest. The side away from the light is in shadow and darker. Use a slightly darker shade of the same color to create shadows.

Draw a burning beam with a color outline instead of the dark ink you used for the robot.

Yellow with white highlights looks golden.

Pure bright colors give a robot a happy look.

Dark grayish colors look like iron or lead.

Use as many colors as you want. For a super silly look, why not try polka dots?

Color Styles

Primary is going to help us get a handle on color styles.

All the robots in this book were colored with a computer. If you would like to do the same, you need to scan your finished drawing after you have traced it with ink and erased any extra lines. Then use an illustration program to choose or create a color and drop it in your drawing.

Paint or pastels are good for blending colors and making blurry shadows. Start with the lighter color first if you plan to layer or blend.

Colored pencils are perfect for making rough textures, blending colors, and shading to create shadows. Use the lighter colors first if you plan to layer or blend.

Markers are easy to use and are best for simple, flat colors—especially bold, bright colors. They're not great for blending colors.

I used markers and colored pencils for this example. Can you tell which is which? You can always mix and match color styles to create exactly the look you want.

Pasting paper cutouts on your robot creates special effects. Don't want to cut teeny, tiny pieces of paper for details like eyes and spindly arms? Draw those details on top of the paper cutouts.

ROBoTs!

Name: _____

Purpose: _____
_____
_____

Hardware: _____
_____
_____

Control Features: _____
_____
_____

Power Source: _____
_____

Special Functions: _____
_____

Data Files: _____
_____
_____
_____
_____

By now your gears should be cranking out inventive ideas for your own collection of functional friends. I don't want you to lose a single android detail or cyborg component. So scan, photocopy, or make your own version of the character sheet to the left. Use one copy for each robot you create and put a sketch or finished drawing in the big white space. Fill in the other blanks with data about your marvelous machine.

List your robot's purpose, special functions, and more. Describe its parts. (Cable-driven locomotion system? Fiberglass body?) Explain its control system. (Silicon cerebral cortex chips? Reprogrammed MP3 player? An auto-destruct code?) Reveal how it's fueled. (Solar panels? Donuts?) Then record your robot's story under Data Files. (How DID you devise such a rad robot, anyhow?)

Final Word

All the instructions in this book are just ideas to get you started. No one—not even the world's most intelligently programmed gizmo—could ever outdo your imagination. So use it to invent your own robots!

Thank You

Thanks to my brother Matthew for letting me test all my crazy robot ideas on him when we were kids.

Index